PRAISE FOR CHRISTINE SLOAN
STODDARD

"With Heaven is a Photograph, Christine Sloan
Stoddard presents you with a poetic meditation on
the fear and desire of making images (and claiming
one's power). Intellectually and spiritually rich, her
words and images imprint on your mind and heart
with beauty, honesty and recognition."

— ART JONES, ARTIST AND FILMMAKER

The narrator of Christine Stoddard's *Heaven is a
Photograph* is hungry. For art. For success. For
salvation. For the weight of a camera in her hands.
She laments that photography is slow to love her
back, which is perhaps what makes this collection so
intoxicating. The unchecked, sometimes fearful and
unabashedly female desire of a woman who cannot
contain her passion—who would let it consume her
—explodes in words and images.

— MARI PACK, AUTHOR OF *DESCRIPTION
OF A NEW WORLD* (DANCING GIRL PRESS)

D0289795

Heaven is a Photograph is a living hagiography of a girl who cannot decide whether or not pursuing photography is a sin. Conflicted by gender expectations and the uncertainty of a career in the arts, the one thing that the protagonist knows is that photography is a deeply spiritual practice, enveloping her life. It is truly an autobiography of many women in the arts.

— GRETCHEN GALES, EXECUTIVE
EDITOR OF QUAIL BELL MAGAZINE

Heaven is a Photograph puts the reader behind, in front of, and inside the camera through Christine Sloan Stoddard's evocative poetry and photography. Through the lens of her viewpoint character, the collection demonstrates the personal and universal appeal of photography in a vivid and impactful manner. Stoddard describes the art of photography as it relates to memory, creation, and legacy in a way that makes the act of clicking the shutter button both an artistic and a spiritual act.

— ALEX CARRIGAN, SENIOR CRITIC AT
QUAIL BELL MAGAZINE

Heaven is a Photograph is a unique exploration of poetry and photography you'll only experience through Christine Sloan Stoddard's magic. The power of her words will shake the core of your being. She doesn't just take pictures—she gives them."

HEAVEN IS A
PHOTOGRAPH

CHRISTINE SLOAN STODDARD

Christine Sloan Stoddard

CL◀SH

For Olivia

CONTENTS

THE DEAD GIRL ARTIST'S SCIENTIFIC METHOD

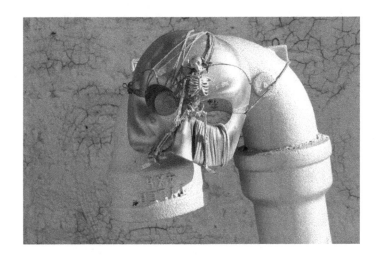

have you ever read
an artist statement
written by a cadaver?
imagine the photographer typing in her coffin.
oh, you thought it was a man?
no, this dead artist is a woman.
some might call her a girl.
she is still willowy.
not yet 30.
never pregnant,
free from the scars
that "make" a "woman."

actually, *was*.

past tense.
she's just a buried body now.

camera mechanics do not intoxicate me
but they enable me to
paint with light.
here in the darkness, I crave light.
in life, I ate too many worms,
too much dirt.
all because he didn't love me.
i shouldn't have cared.
who was he but a ghostly distraction?
a skeletal character too mysterious
for me to add flesh.
you must know a soul
to love it.

i photographed my sallow self before sunset.
these were not expressionistic portraits.
these were scientific documents,
photos for the lab and the archives.

maybe a microscope could tell me
why he did not love me.
I would crack the lens to find out.

was it my curly hair?
did he long for straight?
was it my mayan nose?
did he want a ski slope?
was it my ripe olive tone?
did he prefer peaches and cream?

obsession does not make for

clear thinking
and my mind had always been
crystal.
i should've abandoned my lab coat.
there are softer things to wear.
why live with coarse fabrics?
life is coarse enough.

i probed too hard with my camera.
he doesn't love you.
i stabbed myself with my tripod.
he doesn't love you.
i knocked myself out with studio lights.
he doesn't love you.

an encouraging friend might say:

at least these unrequited affections
taught you photography.
and now you can write
grant proposals from the grave.

is that a nobler use of eternity
than pushing up daisies?
turning rejection and loneliness
into art?

now that I am dead,
my paranoia has died, too.
he never loved me because
he never knew me.
no lab results necessary.

DAUGHTER BEHIND THE LENS

cameras lined the shelves like trophies
and press clippings hung on
his wood panel walls instead
of our family photos

the ghosts of success
the stink of pine

sunday mornings
doused in light and dew
i would worship his name

from the carpeted floor

stiff were the stains
stiff were my legs

my dolls baked like
my mother
they shopped like
my mother

they busied themselves
busy little women

barbies only ever owned
a point-and-shoot
for photo albums
never seen beyond home

their creations
were not
baptized creations

you are the professional
mama told papa
you are the professional

i made my own photo albums
mummified them
in butterfly stickers
but weren't those photo albums
just like barbie's?
pretty pretty pretty
papa's photos were
never pretty

ᴊe like papa?
me

d papa's
ᴊas in secret
ᴇ way you steal
a stroke of the altar

UNREQUITED PIXELS

the weight of a camera
feeds my hungry hands
i can feel the lens breathe
and the shutter beat
like a prudent heart

photography is slow
to love me
but my love races
through valleys
and up mountains
to golden vistas

pining is my pace

y philosophy
wake up in love
i fall asleep in love
and i shoot in love

my memory card
carries portraits
and landscapes
from my soul
to the world

i do not take photos
i give them
as i always give
in love

HIGH SCHOOL PHOTOGRAPHER

playtime is soul food
for the teenage heart

portraits of rebellion
are requisite art projects

youth is fleeting
like photography

hold the camera
same as a cigarette

PORTRAITS OF FRIENDS

humans make contracts
with other humans
but we are animals
who also devour
contracts and spit
them in the woods

paper pulp
carpets the soil
like moss

forget honor
forget clauses
forget policies

signatures are invalid
with beasts
roaming the land

i hold up the camera
and beckon you
to smile
but you can bare
your teeth
any way you choose

PHOTO SNIFFING

my camera seeks
crooked teeth
chapped lips
capillaries

humans are
more photogenic
than cyborgs

MAKER

i envelop toys and trash
with clay
spinning cocoons
from found objects
then i take up
camera and tripod
and march into battle

the battle for moments

the battle for magic

what stories will
i make today?

plant a flag
and capture
the narrative

drama can be small
tiny even
tiny as a spider's eye

i take after insects
and arachnids
i am the hive
the hill
the web

the lens
is my soul
and my exoskeleton

BFA

the tapping of pencils
in the great hall
drums out all serenity
from the brain

think about your
future
my camera is my heart
think about your
life
my camera is my soul
but you have a stomach
feed your stomach

the relentless grip of
societal expectations

could shatter
the skull

i filled out that green
index card
and wrote 'photography'
on the long black line

my major decision was
not so major
right?

the lens obsessed
do not choose
medicine or law
business will not do
dentistry is a cavity
in an artist's heart

we choose the path
that could kill us
pull the trigger
and bang!
goes the camera
ready, set,
shoot

four years and
a diploma
four years and
a portfolio
four years and
nobody knows
what is next

CAMERA FOR COMPANY

do not bring cameras to parties
people want freedom in
their tomfoolery

speaking of toms

CHRISTINE SLOAN STODDARD

peeping toms are
never popular

cameras are for
weirdos
shutterbugs are
weirdos

freshman fifteen
is not a shutter speed
play with your lenses
in your dorm room

you have the same date
every saturday
photography wears
a red dress

WOMB/EYE

the darkroom was
my red home
my red body
my red dreams

crimson water is
a window
and a door

make a picture
make a life

the dorm felt too blue
my eyes were set

for low light

never take a picture
give a picture

this freshman found
refuge in art

beauty is the
perfect sweater
even when it
begins to pill

beauty is
solitude in
the darkroom

parties are imperfect
but you can perfect
a photograph

i became the camera eye
and curled up
in portfolios

i became contact sheets
taped to the wall
i became that image
that burns

HIS GRASP

when he seized my camera
his tongue tore my throat
and my lens cracked

snap a line
snap a life
glass cuts us all

professor dearest
my photos are a poor image
filled with noise
more noise than
my body can muster

soft hums beneath
the crushing weight
of film canisters

or is it grain?
the grain is insane

let's make a movie
we have a flair for trauma
our ghosts will line up
for the picture show

violence is noise
violence is grain

i have loved cinema
since girlhood
almost as much as
i thought i loved you

don't touch me
this camera is mine
i can frame a portrait
i am the portrait
the portrait is me

A MODEL MAKER

my back arches
my shoulders drop
my tongue saddles
the roof of my mouth

posed
poised

i am pleasure
i am spectacle

nude photos pay for college
cleavage for a textbook
nipples erect tripod erect

the camera devours me

in the computer lab
i feast on pixels
square by square
i disappear
wrinkles
freckles
moles
flabs

gone

my mind remains
it always remains
even if only
i see it

RADIANCE CANNOT BE PHOTOSHOPPED

i sit in the digital media lab, swamped by computers with blank faces. the legions sleep— that is, all but one. my computer's screen blinks at me. her impatience clouds the air. i turn away. outside, a snowstorm sweeps across campus. for a moment, i think about the perfection of a single snowflake. then my mind jumps back to silver and white souls humming around me. i tap a random key on the keyboard. the letter 'c.' choose. choose now.

i button up my cardigan and pull my scarf out from my backpack. the lab's large windows make the room an icebox in the winter. the hairs on my arms start to wilt as i warm up. the snow falls harder. down the hall, another student putters around in the kitchen. cabinet doors open and

close. the microwave beeps. that is not my hot food. i
return to my expectant computer. adobe photoshop stares
back at me. *choose.*

tab after tab reveals a woman i have never met. her eyes
pierce my eyes. i do not know her name, her occupation, or
her heart's desires. i only know that i have been tasked with
editing 10 portraits of this person. my professor shared the
portraits via dropbox and included a list of instructions: 1.
remove her freckles. 2. brighten the whites of her eyes.
3. redden her lips. 4. lighten her hair. 5. lessen her chin
waddle. on and on and on.

i do not pity the woman for having bags under her eyes. the
tiny mole on her clavicle does not bother me. her teeth's
slight yellow tint does not make me gasp. in every portrait,
the woman appears happy and health. she smiles not just
with her lips but her whole face. she glows. she knows that
she is loved and that suffering is temporary.

i do a quick color correction on each photo, but only to
adjust for the photographer's errors: underexposure, over-
exposure, blurriness, extraneous visual information that
should be cropped. i do not morph the subject into an
unrecognizable version of herself. as i wait for the files to
upload in my class folder, i compose an email to my
professor explaining why i did not complete the assignment
as required. radiance cannot be photoshopped.

i press send right after the files finish uploading. before i
start to pack up, i glance out the window to the fading
snowstorm.

UNWRITTEN JOB DESCRIPTION

women are photo editors
they edit work by the masters
women do not shoot
because cameras are guns
and we cannot have girls
playing with guns

EXHIBIT

white walls cracked
in strange places
from hammers
and nails
unknown

behold
the vacuum
behold

the cave

i am here to revive you
so breathe

whispers grow into
endless echoes
fail
failure
fail now
fail forever
failure incarnate

the gallery haunts
and taunts me

my studio cowers
and my inner child
weeps from
the floor

all i have to do
is build a kingdom
by myself

HEAVEN IS A PHOTOGRAPH

i am never victorious
except behind the camera
and even then i pray
the atheist who turns
her eyes toward god

30

ACKNOWLEDGMENTS

Thank you to Kaylin Kaupish, Gretchen Gales, Ghia Vitale, Deniz Ataman, and Brian Droitcour.

ABOUT THE AUTHOR

Christine Sloan Stoddard is a Salvadoran-American author, artist, and film/theatre-maker who splits her time between New York City and Virginia. She is the founder of Quail Bell Press & Productions, which recently released *Her Plumage: An Anthology of Women's Writings* From Quail Bell Magazine. Her single author books include *Naomi & The Reckoning, Desert Fox by the Sea, Belladonna Magic*, and other titles. She is a Visible Poetry Project filmmaker, Table Work Press award-winning playwright, and Puffin Foundation emerging artist. She has been the first-ever artist-in-residence at three locations: Lenox Hill Neighborhood House in Manhattan, Brooklyn Public Library-Eastern Parkway Branch, and 1708 Gallery in Richmond, VA. She is a graduate of The City College of New York-CUNY and VCUarts.

Adrian Ernesto Cepeda

REGRET OR SOMETHING MORE ANIMAL
Heather Bell

HELENA
Claire L. Smith

BURIALS
Jessica Drake-Thomas

BROKEN CUP
Jayaprakash Satyamurthy

MARGINALIA
Juno Morrow

SILVERFISH
Rone Shavers

NO NAME ATKINS
Jerrod Schwarz

THE ELVIS MACHINE
Kim Vodicka

WE PUT THE LIT IN LITERARY

CLASHBOOKS.COM

FOLLOW ON TWITTER, IG & FB

@clashbooks